There is No Pressure Like a Heart in a Dam

poems by

Jennifer Weber

Finishing Line Press
Georgetown, Kentucky

There is No Pressure Like a Heart in a Dam

Copyright © 2022 by Jennifer Weber
ISBN 978-1-64662-811-7 First Edition
All rights reserved under International and Pan-American Copyright Conventions. No part of this book may be reproduced in any manner whatsoever without written permission from the publisher, except in the case of brief quotations embodied in critical articles and reviews.

ACKNOWLEDGMENTS

Dedicated to my grandfather, who always believed I would have a poetry collection one day.

Publisher: Leah Huete de Maines
Editor: Christen Kincaid
Cover Art: Lindsay Campbell
Author Photo: Lindsay Campbell
Cover Design: Elizabeth Maines McCleavy

Order online: www.finishinglinepress.com
also available on amazon.com

Author inquiries and mail orders:
Finishing Line Press
PO Box 1626
Georgetown, Kentucky 40324
USA

Table of Contents

Not a Morning for Weeping 1

Birdsong 2

Ode to Tea Leaves 3

Perennial 4

Monet's Water Lilies 5

Our Last Summer in Cape May 6

Stones 7

Open House 8

Sisterhood 9

Self-Determination 10

Migration Patterns 11

Hiraeth 12

Andean Lungs 13

to the southwest deserts 14

River People 15

Disillusion 16

There is No Pressure Like a Heart in a Dam 18

Sacrifice Dream 19

Dry Spells 20

Things to Ask a Man at a Bar 21

Penelope in the Morning, Many Years Later 22

A Car Travels Further When It's Running On Spite 23

How to Pick Up a Poem 24

Not a Morning for Weeping

I am glad to wake up to rain. Cold
water carrying its own secrets, ribbons
of ponderous clouds. Muscles
pleasantly heavy and nothing to push
me out of bed. Beneath a smudge of leftover
dreams, gratification slipping indistinct
between raindrops, I do not need to wring
my hands. The dishwasher in my apartment
is broken and I've never fixed anything
without first asking for help. My cousin
is praised for her new job, my father
for his retirement, and the last time
I tried to grow houseplants I came home
to rings of dead leaves. For now it is better
to be here, stretching through this respite,
bare youth against soft quilts. I do not compete
with the rest, who only know glory
when sunshine greets their skin.

Birdsong

Quick as a dream releases me at dawn
they flit through the backyard, slivered
wings in my periphery. Feet wrapped gentle
around branches, beaks open
in noisy delight. In the morning
they wake me and I want to say
to the wren, *tell me about your songs.*
I want to perch alongside the cardinal, lay
soft fingers against his red crest. Ask the bluejay,
how do you carry so much joy in your breast?
Everything I sing in the shower
only slips down the drain and sometimes
when I sleep my chest feels so heavy.
Show me your tiny, beating hearts,
I'd say. *Teach mine how to flutter.*

Ode to Tea Leaves

Your ceramic mug handle
arching leisurely
against my palm. Almost
too hot to hold but
I persist because you
are morning ritual,
unsweetened yet delightful.
Oh, to watch your steam
unfolding like butterfly wings!
Your small tag on thin string
resting in delicate languor
over a rim, graceful
model of relaxation!
With you, I can spend time
in small sips. Maybe
no makeup on yet. Maybe
nothing prepared for breakfast.
What joy there is, to pause
with you before routine
hurtles me into the day!
I can contemplate new sunlight
on my shins. I can hope
you'll share a new future,
waiting to be read
in the bottom of your mug.

Perennial

Last year we saw the first of them
together. Daffodils bent in a gentle greeting,
curved beneath the wooden park sign.
Sitting on a bench, I counted petals
that grew the way I wanted to—
open and brave and unapologetic.
I could tell you were thinking
about rejuvenation: a stream
returning to life, new grass appearing
on our grandfather's grave. Sister,
tell me when you see them again.
Think of me when you recognize
our mother in the winter-cracked skin
of your knuckles and call me back
to that park bench. I'll bring
your coffee and a gentle breeze, some
comfortable silence. On the brink
of spring, we can be perennial too.

Monet's Water Lilies

Your long canvas hangs like an embrace
meant for me, alone in a room
on the fifth floor of a quiet art museum.

I study your overlapping
brushstrokes and think they look
like secrets. Delicate but
deliberate. Lily pads floating
among shades of blue
I do not know the names of.

You call out to the water
I carry within me, life
and tears and shifting tides.
Immersing myself in your reflections
of light on water, I think of the womb
I came from and the one
I haven't yet filled. You
offer a surface I wish I could
see beneath, a beauty
I wish I could cup in my hands.

Our Last Summer in Cape May

Facing west, I sit quiet beneath sunset
colors. Pieces of white paint peel away

from the roof deck railing and a still-damp towel
rests over the back of my chair, cool against my shoulders.

Two boys moving in tandem race on bikes
around the block, bodies lifted above seats,

supple backs curved over handlebars. They chase
bits of sunlight around the corner, again

three minutes later, and again, and for now I know
there is a pattern to my future. In this comfort

I lick faint salt from my lips. It is simple to hear a new
lullaby in the curling of waves. Easy to pretend

this evening can last as long as I wish, a humidity
never broken by storms. In the wide street below

bicycle spokes rush past and spit sand, propelled
by pale legs flashing strips of youth in the dusk.

Stones

In front of me, your tombstone.
In my hand, a rock I chose.
Perfectly round except a nick
at the top where I press
my thumb against sharp edges,
scratching delicate skin beneath my nail.

Neither stone understands how
you died and I cannot remember.
Grandmother, do you know
how often my uncle cried? If
my father ever woke in the night,
Hebrew funeral prayers
in shrouds on his tongue?

Maybe I have your fingers, maybe
your chin. Looking at the stones
placed by my uncle and father
I wonder if they hide something
secret and tender in their centers.
Something I can pull out
from between tissues and tendons.

I lay my rock on top of your tombstone
alongside the others. A shameful offering,
a tentative question.

Open House

When all is settled at the end of day,
glass windows open in rooms now empty—
we wait. No ghosts remain to make us stay.

Old photos covered though still on display.
Lamplight muted, we cross floorboards gently
when all is settled at the end of day.

In closets we search for relics and pray,
hope they still exist. Held by vacancy
we wait. No ghosts remain to make us stay.

Proud figures once stood, tall in doorways.
Now we are left with rooms of memory
when all is settled at the end of day.

We linger, try to box up new dismay,
more quiet than we ever thought we'd be.
We wait. No ghosts remain to make us stay.

Beneath stairs, shadows stretch in shades of gray.
Missing what we can neither hold nor see,
when all is settled at the end of day
we wait. No ghosts remain to make us stay.

Sisterhood

This is what I think of when you ask me for truth.

The marvel of our cheekbones
exposing identical frameworks to the mirror.

Youth we wore like sundresses,
hued the same color as shared blood.

Brown eyes laughing into blue.

Chins tilted in the same direction,
a subtle sweep when we know we're lying.

A jawline in your mirror, conjuring
my mouth when I speak in anger.

The tightening when the words do not come.

Self-Determination

The invitation of an open seat faces
a desert horizon line, the long stretch of afternoon.

Above, the silhouette of a hawk against
an empty sky. Red dust around your ankles.

Across the table sits a stranger, your father.
The coincidence, the purposeful. Which is to say

the genetics. No shade to spare at high noon
but your future must come from somewhere, drawn

from the pause before laying down a new card.
In your hand, all the kings keep looking back.

On your wrist, a watch that just started to work.
You've always been a gambler but

the next card feels like it could be your last.
Maybe it's always been up your sleeve.

Migration Patterns

At dinner, I watch your knuckles tighten
around your fork. We don't eat dessert

together anymore and I haven't felt
your knees pressed against mine in weeks.

In February we tried migration.
We aimed for a tropical escape but

while packing our socks we rolled
up our issues, and like birds

ended up back where we started.
In the morning, you begin to leave

notes. *Be back soon*—and always the time
you expect to come home. A full year

of seasons within a day: your return,
our nesting, the next inevitable absence.

Hiraeth
> *Welsh, noun: a homesickness for a home that you can't return to or never was.*

It is nighttime. The train station
rests empty and hollow and you sit
in its center. A backpack, plus a jacket
that looks like something you might
have worn at home. You think you remember
it as a place with green shutters, maybe
petunias by the mailbox. Dark cabinets
in the kitchen or perhaps that image
came from a movie. Tall elms you passed
this morning reminded you of an open
backyard but that might not be quite
right either. You watch someone
else's train fly by, singing "*Hiraeth,
hiraeth,*" as it passes over steel tracks,
a bit of homesickness caught between its wheels.

Andean Lungs

While hiking in the Andean mountains
a spirit kept pace with me
from within the clouds. She looked
like I imagined my soul would:
weightless and surrounded
by mountains, sometimes a heart
pierced through by their peaks.

One night I climbed
as high as my lungs allowed
and called out,
asked why she willingly
suffered those jagged rocks.
She answered: After my blood
runs down to the river
it is returned to me,
valley mists rising,
and I press myself
against sharp peaks
to feel everything once more.

to the southwest deserts

at sunrise, your baked and placated fires
the roads that meander through you
cars that point toward your horizons
the dust you leave in their crevices
secrets that emerge beneath your uninterrupted stars
the history you give us in layers of sand and clay
your misleading distances
precious blooms and hidden warnings
your sparse and open expanses
waiting for the wind to sweep through
for the rivers to return
a lover coming to lie down
in the space between your mountains

River People

On our mountain a fire tried
to consume us, an out of control benediction.
To save ourselves we descended
deep into a valley, fell in love
with its river. Caught more fish
than we could carry and drank wine
made of grapes grown plump from its water,
wandering away one night with
full baskets and stained lips. Years later
we still wear scales linked in necklaces,
threaded through our hair.
Passed-down reminders of a river
that could never wait in one place
for us, a futile kind of inheritance.

Disillusion

Begin with an empty metropolis,
one without neighborhoods or street signs.
Collect bits left behind by people
that lived there before you—

a dog leash, mismatched gloves.
Folders of committee minutes
you can't decipher. A crown
that fits on your head.

Sit overlooking your city. Forget
the moon and its light and
everything it's ever done for you.
Find a king and drag him down

to warm a throne at your side.
Promise him ocean views,
room for a dog. Ask his name
but know you'll forget it.

Collect mannequins. Assign them jobs
and name them subjects. Melt them
down to plastic when you become jealous
of their posture and blank faces.

Refuse to place candles in dark rooms.
Consider what your old therapist would say
but decide it doesn't matter
and keep all matches in your fists.

One morning your king will ask
about recycling the mannequins
you destroyed. He'll want to talk
about forming new committees,

cleaning up your streets. Tell him
you'll take notes. Instead, leave before
too much dawn slips between buildings
and knocks the crown off your head.

There is No Pressure like a Heart in a Dam

This could never be a gradual release. I carry
the darkness of deep waters and you

hold onto wishes hung around your neck:
a selection of pennies, a horseshoe on a chain.

A scarab beetle from your mother. You hope
their fortune will help you float. We rise

as if from confessional but I never opened
my mouth. Behind my lips, the force

of unnamed desires. I still hold a reservoir and I
can sink more wishes, can flood many mornings yet

Sacrifice Dream

On a wooden porch facing the edge of a forest,
we are the only animals that haven't fled.

Tinder is collected beneath cushions
and coffee tables. Cabinets are packed

with clusters of old leaves. In a rising heat
we know rotten floorboards will give in first

so we spend the day removing nails,
slipping molten metal into each other's veins.

Tiny pieces of bones and scraps
of burnt clothing blow toward us on

dry wind. We forgot every god's name
and never prayed for forgiveness.

By tomorrow evening our hair will smell of smoke.
By tomorrow evening we will lie down with ash.

Dry Spells

It is my desire to understand
one another perfectly.

The space between us a cactus.
The only time I admit thirst

is when I hold a clogged spigot.
Around your neck, a lock

I cannot pick. Too many teeth
and the biting inevitable.

At high noon my dress falls apart,
paperclips waiting in pockets.

Water held in the hem. Your hands
erupt from dry soil, seeds beneath

nails. Rust from cuticles.
We sow dandelions

and queen's lace, grow our
weeds covered in cactus spines.

Things to Ask a Man at a Bar

Who do I remind you of, sitting in profile on a barstool?
Do you miss your family, your first car?
Do you miss yesterday already?
Do you tell the same story over and over
        but change the ending every time?
Do you talk in your sleep? Will anyone respond?
Have you ever left a bar in the middle of a beer and known
        it was the last time you'd be there?
Do you wake up and know which way is east?
Do you notice my lies? Do you know your own?
Do you think we'd recognize each other, suddenly on the same
        street corner, squinting under an August afternoon sun?
Is there a question you've never had to answer? Which is to say—
        how often do you get something for free?

Penelope in the Morning, Many Years Later

No matter how many times they've moved,
the shape of Odysseus's body against their sheets
still reminds her of Ithaca's coastline.

She lies in bed, devotion coating her tongue
like a badly aged wine and waits
for him to wake up. She wants to argue.
She does not want to hold out her hands
in welcome, hostess to another weekend party.

The alcohol may have improved but
men still ask for the same stories,
cattle to Charybdis, listening while they play
lawn games. The women always talking
about DIY crafts while trying to spot her loom.

Centuries later and her name still means weaver.

She is restless, tired of waiting. When she rises
to get dressed she'll have to pass the bow, hanging
next to his suits. Odysseus wanted it displayed
over the mantel but she wanted it burned,
so this seems like a compromise
their marriage counselor will call progress.

Easy enough to talk about her desperation
preserved in the curve of his bow. Pleading speeches
and anxious fidelity, the violence that followed
her final trick. Something she hasn't admitted
yet: she hates that it still reminds her
of how easily she fell in love, thinking
about Odysseus drawing back the string,
muscles shifting under the sun.

A Car Travels Further if it's Running on Spite

You don't even need
a suitcase. Just half a tank
and your ex's voice in your ear
the way it always hovered, following
you out of the bedroom, lingering
above the coffee pot and plates of fruit
he never wanted to share.

On your way east, thinking
about breakfast, you stop
to stretch your legs at a farm stand.
Satisfaction on display,
clustered in globes of oranges,
ripe with a slight give beneath
your fingertips. Plump in your hands.

It's been eighty-seven miles
and the needle hasn't dipped.
In your passenger seat
sits a brown paper bag,
heavy and full, trailing
a faint sticky-sweet scent
out the window.

How to Pick Up a Poem

With condensation on your fingertips,
too much pale skin in the corner
of your eye. Confessions slowly
discarded. Muscles heavy as you move
through spaces crowded with murky
words, distracted by bright tips
of cigarettes and a sense of displacement.
You could find some writing on the
walls, a disjointed ending, maybe
something smudged and prophetic
behind a beautiful woman's barstool.
Cut yourself off and head home
instead. Wake tomorrow with a broken
glass still in your hand. Bleed a bit
of metaphor, dark and amber like last
night's whiskey on the back of your throat.

Jennifer Weber holds a degree in English literature from Bucknell University and has been writing creatively since she was a young girl. She has lived and worked in New York City for many years and she loves a good thunderstorm, bread fresh out of the oven, and family lawn games. Weber's poetry has previously appeared in various literary journals and poetry magazines, including *Inwood Indiana Press, Slipstream Press,* and *Eastern Iowa Review.*

www.ingramcontent.com/pod-product-compliance
Lightning Source LLC
LaVergne TN
LVHW040118080426
835507LV00041B/1767